The Mix
The Evolution of the Pen and Pad

The Mix is a collection of writings befitting for all readers. It is mental stimulation at its finest; A true page turner. Think about your favorite mix tape or album. The first time you popped it in you didn't know what was going to bless your ears. Well the Evolution of the Pen & Pad is just that.

Poetically triggering all emotions as you go on a poetic journey with the author. If you enjoy empowerment, love, eroticism, liberation, comedy and the dark side of poetry. *The Mix:Evolution Of The Pen & Pad* has it all.

I dedicate this masterpiece of words to the beautiful souls who have supported me from the very start. The beings that make up my amazing tribe, that pushed me when I greatly needed to be pushed. For the dreamer that dared to dream and made it a reality, I give this to you.

For the person that clapped, snapped and cheered for my poems because they loved my art, I dedicate this to you.
I hope you all enjoy this book as much as you adore your favorite CD or mixtape.

Peace and Blessing to all,
Sharita Renee

Table of Contents

9 Evolution of the Pen and Pad
11 Black Butterfly
13 Anything for the High
15 You Woke My Crazy Bitch Up
17 Black Woman Shit

18 Don't Leave Me Behind
21 Community Dick
22 Wet Pillowcase
23 Extraordinary Beings
25 AVN Award Worthy

26 Who Mad?
29 I Might be in a Sunken Place
31 Cold Sweet Potato Pie
33 Stay
36 G

38 Wet Kanda Dream
39 Is it me?
40 On the set
41 I'm in Need of His Poetry
42 Thief

43 Tongue Tied
44 Black Woman's Tool Belt
45 Universal Guardians
46 Apart of Your World
47 Inspirational Stroke

26. Can't Get Right
27. Good Lotion
28. Sunflower Amongst Roses
29. A Queen Doesn't Have To Take
30. Painted smiles

31. Make Up Sex
32. My Mister
33. She Still Sleeps Alone
34. Who is Sharita Renee?
35. Misrepresenting

36. Laugh Now Cry Later
37. Perfection Surrounded by Imperfection
38. Christmas Gift
39. Chessboard
40. Orange Jumpsuit

41. Shit Mixed Shit
42. Go Fund Me
43. Woman to Female
44. Mother May I?
45. Pedestal

46. No Wings
47. Family in the Sky
48. Three Way
49. Fatal
50. Hell on Earth

51. All That Talking
52. Return My Heart
53. Somebody Else's King
54. Let's Grow Old Together
55. Bloody Words

56. Day Dreaming
57. Carnivorous
58. Earthly Father
59. Good Enough

49 Cant Get Right
50 Good Lotion
51 Sunflower Amongst Roses
53 A Queen Doesn't Have to Take
55 Painted Smiles

58 Make Up Sex
67 My Mister
68 She Still Sleeps Alone
69 Who is Sharita Renee
70 Misinterpreting

72 Laugh Now Cry Later
74 Perfection Surrounded by Imperfection
76 Christmas Gift
78 Chessboard
79 Orange Jumpsuit

80 Shit Mixed Shit
81 Go Fund Me
83 Woman to Female
85 Mother May I
87 Pedestal

89 No Wings
91 Family in the Sky
92 Threeway
93 Fatal
94 Hell on Earth

96 All That Talking
98 Return My Heart
99 Somebody Else's King
101 Lets Grow Old Together
102 Bloody Words

104 Day Dreamin'
105 Carnivorous
106 Earthly Father
108 Good Enough
109 I Wish She Had a Dick

111 Fuck Your Brother
112 Fucking or What
114 I'm Gone
115 Something About His Eyes
117 Meat Delivery

119 The Great

121 About The Author

The Mix: Evolution of the Pen and Pad

Evolution of the Pen and Pad

Rita Renee!
"Flip that tape over for me niece"
My uncles used to jam, I mean them joints were hard
Pulling up in the Monte Carlo
Unc rocking the high top fade
these memories will never age

I was at peace
Heading to school in Dunjee
The pleasures of being a young country kid
Pen and paper in hand
No I don't want it in my back pack
Trying to write before I could even spell
Caution to the wind, what the hell?

I know what I'm trying to say tho'
Me myself and I, let's write
My imagination was so far out,
I'd forget when it was time to get out
Crying,
not understanding why I'm getting dropped off here

Day twenty three
but every day is a new day to me
I just want to go home
to play with my dolls,
my voice has the ability to change
I have a voice for all forty six plus.

The evolution of the pen and pad
The growth of the voiceless that had many voices
Story teller not a liar
My mouth piece is dire
Jones born, Spencer raised

I have seen some things
Oh my, how thangs have changed
With many voices for the voiceless,
I have found that peace
Flip that tape from side A to B, niece!

Black Butterfly

I stood there
In the middle of a dark room
moonlight from a window
Revealing the night
With a faint scent of death lingering

What the hell am I doing here?
What happened?
My hands shaking
Body aching

I killed her
Oh my god, I killed her
I've been talking about this day forever
Planning and plotting
Never ever would I have imagined,
I would have the guts to follow through

I had to murder the old me
Give her that eternal sleep
In that dark room highlighted by the moon
I put the gun of self-love to my head
Pulled the trigger
And allowed the self-hate to pour from me

I killed her
The hurt and the pain from what's his name. POW!
The body shame. POW!
Black Bitch ain't my name. POW!
Raped as a teen. POW!
Two baby daddies,
You won't amount to anything
POW! POW!

My worst enemy was me
It took more than one bullet to kill the old me

Anything for the High

My mother sold my innocence
when I was only six
For a small piece of rock,
How does that make sense?

Guess the apple don't fall far from the tree.
Weed alone never did it for me.
I needed that type of high that would numb and ease my pain
For that type of high, I would do anything.

My family disowned me.
Stealing from grandma's purse
before she would head out for church,
Was the first time I took from a loved one.

I just needed a hit so bad.
But my luck ran out,
after doing this so much,
grandma kicked me out.

Coke up my nose,
Heroin shot through my veins.
I'd go without eating
but not without my drugs mayne.

I remember when
I had just enough meat left on my bones to turn tricks.
See when I was a youngster my mother taught me this...

A women is never broke,
it's a gold mine between your thighs
And the highest bidder
gets the sweetest piece of your pie.
The things I did for a twenty,

would make you sick
Fifty to one hundred
you couldn't get more sinful than this.

I'm better off dead
a junkie that won't quit.
I'd sell my soul to the tambourine man for a hit.

In and out of rehab,
Just to get out and go right back to the streets.
How will I ever get clean?
My scariest nightmare is also my happiest dream.

Will I never get clean?
From birth I was cursed,
just another crack baby.

What would my life be like?
If momma never picked up that crack pipe,
To ease the pain of her uncle raping her
at night?

She was just a child,
Grandma called her fast,
Said she shouldn't have been twisting and shaking her little ass.
Drugs were her escape.
In a world where sunshine doesn't come
but it always rains.
Heart full of rage 'cause no one cares about your pain.

I understand how my mother could
Sale me for that rock.
But I don't understand how this cycle
will ever stop.

You Woke my Crazy Bitch Up

You love me?
Oh you love me?
I think you don't even know what love means
See history got me in a bind
You done played me like a fucking fool too many times
With your bold face lies

No wonder why this other hoe a nut
You fueling the nutty bitch's bus
now I got to cuss
Because you really got me fucked up
I'm sitting on my hands
'cause I really want to bust yo' ass up

While others are tit I'm just tat
Bring me some shit
I'ma throw you some back
Tat tat motherfucking tat
I don't have time to fall back

I'm all the way in and you my friend
About to go for a spin
A long ass ride
Bushes and trees darkness outside
Shut that crying shit up
I can hear you through the trunk

The bugs can feast on your sorry ass
Like you feasted on my emotions
Devoured my time
Played me
And shamed my love
That's a hate crime

So now let's play
Cause guess who got free time
Black Storm
Black Widow
Black Plague
Be my name

You done woke my crazy bitch up
She's in fucking rage
You about to be front page news
Another cheating dead ass dude
You ripped my heart out
So I took my time as I cut out yours

Since you with that snake shit
You can resemble one
Slit your tongue down the middle just for fun
Since you like pussy so much
I will use my scissors and scalpel to make you one
Goodbye dick!

Snip Snip
9-1-1, what's your emergency?
I'd like to report a murder
365 x 2
Stab wounds
One shot to the head
Oh yeah he's dead

You asked who did it
That crazy bitch went back to sleep
She can now slumber in peace
You woke her up

So it's only right
That your departure sound effects
Become her newest lullaby
Rocking her back to sleep
Isn't it funny how music calms the beast?

Black Woman Shit

My black is purely untainted
you can be mad that I'm a child of the sun
and my complexion complements the night sky
my woolly hair is my crown
and I give no fucks when you stare me down
My head is up high

My hips are classified as wide
you can see my smile from either side
If you must stare, get my good side
I'm bottom heavy, this I know
but that doesn't mean you have the right to proceed
To highjack things that were genetically given to me

so will we keep pretending that the black woman isn't the beginning,
the end and all things in between
She is the reason for all the bomb ASS trends
she might of came from he
but she is more than just of his rib
And protector of his heart

you are amongst the most beautiful creatures on Earth
how dare you play us like we have no worth
We are as rich as the soil
we are one with Mother Earth
from our minds, to our lips, to our hips to the bottom of our feet
we can give you heaven on Earth
But it's up to you to receive

Don't Leave me Behind

My love for the black man will never deteriorate
Tho' we've been through somethings designed to rip us apart
You thought I didn't support your dreams
But I worked late night shifts for us
When you ran out on me it was tough

Although the blow knocked me down
I found my footing and got back up
I healed

He wasn't the him for me
Yet I prefer to love unconditionally
He is a reflection of me
While other women are taught
they need a man
Black women are taught
we don't need one at all

That we can be overly independent and strong
you were meant to breed, then to be on your own
Bullshit!

On the shores of west Africa
Cape Coast Castles
They didn't capture slaves
We were humans
Living our lives freely
Mothers, fathers, sisters, brothers,
husbands, wives, a tribe
Don't play us like we were not civilized

Script from our culture, language, our worship
Bond with chains
We were free before they hit our shores
Nobody understands the essence of a black woman

like her black man
We don't have to say a thang,
just gaze into my eyes and nod
Yea' yea' we on the same page
We are mute to some situations
Because our connection is that strong
There isn't a soul on this earth that will protect you
like a Nubian Queen can

Take me by the hand
and allow our exchange of energy to take place
We have recused each other from the sunken place
I need you, you need me
We have already been together don't you see
No matter how many times we get it wrong
With the right one we will get it right

As we dance
Invoking the ancestors
As we gyrate under the stars
We put the Willie Lynch letter to shame
Buried the slave mentality
where it will never be Resurrected again

Hey lover
Our story didn't begin in bondage
We were somebody and we still are
If we live life in four cycles
then him and I have already connected
We've been soulmates at least twice

converting sugar canes
into pure sugar or rum,
Picking cotton in the fields
just maybe we were a part of a dynasty,
With not a care in the world,
Yet in each phase of life tho' we were in different bodies
our energy remained the same
the connection brought us together each time
Just maybe, just maybe

we are a part of some unique design
Individually we are amazing
together we are spectacular
United we are the most powerful force,
Indeed superior you are

Don't forget about me
Because together we are free
What was once a nightmare
We have flipped to a dream
Elevated and made a reality
You and me must never part
The most high put us together from the very start

Shake me from my slumber
You are awakened too
We are on the run to real freedom
And I'm not leaving you

Community Dick

Sit yo' hot dick ass down,
Don't long for me to be in your arms and be around
You make me sea sick
just let me drown
While you fucking anything with a hole being a fucking clown
You Community dick,
so I guess everybody hitting now

Thought you wanted to be that exclusive dick,
let that shit simmer now,
She can be stank breath,
ugly in the face and bad bodied,
And stupid enough to think
she won't run around OKC telling everybody

That's the description of these revolving doe hoes you be sliding in,
Then coming in with that bum ass line...
"Queen I'm single, them just my friends
you can meet 'em sometime."
Negro done lost his damn mind...

Where that committed dick at?
That only want to be in yo' shit dick at,
That on god you the only one hitting this dick at,
Where that mindset to match dick?
so I can grab my Chap stick
Sing on his mic the sweetest song
when it goes down long
This performance here ain't for your camera phones
Just something to put on yo' dome,
on the ride home

Don't get me wrong I love the magic stick,
But get out my face and space with that
Community dick

Wet Pillowcase

I hope this is my last heartbreak.
I pray these are the last tears I ever cry,
Over a love that was never truly mine.
I never cheated or lied,
I put my best foot forward and always tried.
From the very beginning the road was rocky
But I couldn't allow for that to stop me.
I thought I seen greatness in his eyes.
Yet so many times he showed me I was blind.
Keep on fighting...
You love him, don't you?
Then keep on fighting.
Hell, I'm in the ring by myself.
I don't have any more tears left.
I loved you through your pain,
only for you to 'cause me pain.
What did I gain?
Besides a broken heart and new love scars.
I loved you even when you didn't know how to love me.
I gave you my heart and you fumbled it purposely

Extraordinary Beings

We were doing extraordinary things
Before they even crawled out the caves
You're only a threat when you're powerful
Nobody's worrying about someone
they don't see as Superior
You don't need Wikipedia
To tell you, who you really are
My elders been spitting the truth
it's up to us to embody and embrace

Our greatness
Too woke!
Too loud!
Too proud!
Too bold!
Too Black!
Add too fed up to all that

Black boys getting taught to hate black girls
Black girls being taught they don't need black boys
So we encounter black men and women that can't love their own
So then what happens to black family?
What becomes of Black love?
This is the hellish blow that will wipe us out
and we aren't ready to bow out, so
Check this out
we are pushing our black agenda even harder

Black family!
Black love!
Black Marriage!
Black business!
Black Pride!

Black men we need you and you need us to,
no matter what we go through we still got you
Show us that y'all still have our backs too

It's too many Baby daddies and not enough husbands
Too many baby mothers and not enough wives
We are wasting too much time and energy
On meaningless soul ties and late nights
Bump and grinds that leave us hollow inside

It starts with us and ends with us
Believe in your greatness,
let's really step up!
If you're down for the change,
put your fist up!

AVN Awards Worthy

It's like butter baby...
That's all I could hear in the background
As he pounded my womb into submission.
He has the right to be cocky,
dick on champ mode call him rocky.
I'm all the way in when I'm giving him sloppy toppy.

He has a balanced diet.
As he ejaculated, his sweet dick juices filled my mouth.
My immune system smiled as I swallowed every drop.
Who needs *One a Days*?
When good dick keeps the doctor away
My diet all beef
that foot long he presented was more than enough for me,
Combination of salty and sweet.

Yea, that's my shawty and he can get it 365.
Give my pussy CPR, oh she still alive.
Call a camera man, let's make a movie baby.
Glad I'm rocking my natural,
pull that shit as you insert the tip.
Gone and lay my body down,
in these juices you might drown.
I'm not even trying to clown,
in a good pussy contest I'd be crowned.

Momma didn't raise no hoe but in the bedroom I'm hoe 4.0
Climax as I throw it back allow these yams to fully smack.
It's like butter baby,
now sounds like thunder claps.
All this ass bouncing on your lap.
We gave each other daps,
a round of applause and finger snaps.
Roll the credits!

Who Mad?

I'm just sitting with my piece
When this fine ass brother
Flops down next to me
Irritated is an understatement
Oh he pissed

I'm a firm believer in
'Mind yo' own damn business'
So I continued to follow my golden rule
"Why the fuck black women get so mad
when they see us with white women?"

I looked around
Yep I'm the only Nubian around.
So he talking to me,
I'm super black woman

Black like not giving a fuck
when I see you with a Neanderthal walking hand and hand
Black like let freedom ring,
while you give praise to ivory things
Black like, fro's out fists up

I asked the brother,
"Do you want the truth?"
Because if your prepared, I will tell you.
With his brows turned up he replied "yes."
this topic gives me not one tea spoon of stress.

We put sap on your backs
when Massa thought you even looked Susan's way.
Washed your bodies in herbs and flowers
after cutting you down from tall trees.
They hung you by the necks
Beat and castrated you

after false accusations from Mrs. Stringy hair
that you raped her.
Lie after lie,
Ms. Thang screaming, "Die nigger die!"
But you don't hear that anymore.

Black body's swinging
we were there.
Fast forward, y'all shot down in the streets.
Those mad black women,
protesting by the thousands.
Your lives matter to them, even before it's taken.

Where are your pale faced queens?
The ones you praise over all things...
Who's mad?
Black like the night,
when the Most High created life.
Black like Assata Shakur,
enduring abuse in a males prison for a crime she didn't commit

Your black life matters to us.
For you we put up a fuss.
Who mad?
I say, who mad?
The ones that struggle with you,
Build you up to your greatness, only to get dumped.

Who mad, king?
The most unprotected
the most disrespected
Head up high, most neglected.

Yet the most beautiful beings to ever grace the planet.
Who mad? Not us!
Matter of fact get yo' ass up.
I looked him in the eyes and spoke life into him.
I don't know what Black Queen hurt you,
but push through.
Come what may, we still love you.

When you see a black woman,
try speaking and giving a smile.
You know that same all teeth smile,
You give when you see those same white women
you think we're mad at
Yea king, try that.

I Might be in the Sunken Place

At some point you have to be all in or all the way out.
Can't get time back and we truly need to treat it as that.
Don't block someone's view
because you have yet to see the greatness,
that's worthy of love too.

I heard that there's no feeling like being in love
with someone that's in love with you,
Is that true?
I'm just wondering after all this time
why are we still at step one commitment wise?
Yet have surpassed all steps physically.

See I'm too good at staying in my lane
going with the flow just riding the wave,
Because as time has passed you have grown on me.
JaRule voice you not just my lover, you my homie.
To tell the truth if I cut you loose
I'm going to be hurting too,
Not knowing what to do
but at some point this will have to do.

Time, time, time don't keep wasting time.
You're hurt, I get it.
You loved and it got ignorant.
But how long you going to live in it?

The universe trying to give you who you need,
but you won't allow your heart to heal
so that you can proceed.
So this is my creed,
Love me in the now.
Allow me to be the one
With no push backs.

I'm not her and she ain't me and that's facts.
No more promises you can't keep
No more dates that you can't meet
Either be all in or be all out
You got to release me
even if you don't know how

Cold Sweet Potato Pie

See I remember late nights up in my grandma's kitchen
She always said things that were so interesting
We would converse about life but mostly about men
One statement always took the grand stand
What can you do for a man that no other woman can?

Any woman can make a meal
Bear some children
Work like a mule
But that's not what has kept your grandfather here
So what are you going to do that sets you above the rest?
When infidelity creeps in, will you think you're less?
Are you strong enough to ride out the storm?

Who is the weak one?
The woman who leaves,
Or the one who stays and never strays?
These statements alone weighed heavy on my mental
'Til one night I had an answer
While eating cold sweet potato pie at the table
My grandma looked me in the eyes
with a grin on her face and said,
"What can you do for a man that no other woman can?"

I placed my fork down ready to speak my truth
Well G-mama I'm a one and not a two
Competition there is none
He want to go, then have fun
She can give him some cat
But I'm the lioness that's going to bring him peace
When the weight of the world is on his shoulders
I'm his stress relief, his P.I.C
His rock and whenever he wants to give up
I won't allow him to

All kings weren't meant to rule
but it's his birth right
I will carry him to the throne if I have to
Submitting because he showed me he is worthy to submit to
There are endless amounts of things I can do

But the man that's for me
will bring all this to the table too
A woman is as good as her man
And vice versa

Love, Loyalty and respect
Aren't hard to give
I'm willing to fight the good fight
But will he?
If infidelity creeps in
I won't split his scalp
Because losing me will be the mightiest blow, no doubt

I don't doubt storms will come
I won't turn and run
But he has to know he is the moon,
amongst many shining stars
But my beacon of light is like no other
Going against what God has given him
Will make his entire world plunder

I picked up my fork
and started back eating my cold sweet potato pie
My grandmother stood,
as she cut me another slice of pie
"You know what baby
You're going to be alright."

Stay

Singing: *But why don't you stay?*
I'm down on my knees.
I'm so tired of being lonely
Don't I give you what you need?
When they call, you to go...
there is one thing you should know
We don't have to live this way...
Baby, why don't you stay?

He says I argue 'bout the same ol' bullshit!
You got damn right!
You keep doing the same dumb shit
then wonder why we fight.
But you have amnesia;
call yo' mom with that same slick ass month,
See if she will feed ya.

I'm in cardiac arrest from the heart attacks you gave me,
When I said I'd stay...
you turned around and played me.
I want to rip you to pieces,
but I'd only put you right back together.
I remember when I truly thought we'd be together forever.

I'm at your throat because you're dead wrong.
I wanted to make this house a home but now
I don't even want to come home.
I used to look at you and see God.
How you'd grab me by my waist and plant sweet kisses
All over my face,
just to start off our day.

Shit I'd be in class thinking about you.
You and I been down since junior high school.

It was all fun and games
you were so in love.
'Til we got pregnant.
Before we seen that positive piss test
you were talking marriage.
I couldn't even think about aborting our baby.
Tears in my eyes from you trying to plant the seed of doubt,
We were kids having kids, no doubt.

Together I never questioned our abilities.
Lifetime movie, *shhh our real life show is on.*
I love you but you make me so mad,
at times I don't even recognize you.
I know you married me because of the baby
But I thought love would always get us through.
Would I be lying if I said I'm not madly in love with you?

As time ticks, feeling like I should just let you go.
You're not happy, I'm not happy
What happened to the rhythm to my flow?
What makes it even worse?
You let this outside hoe know
Pillow talking about our problems with everybody but me.
I used to think I wasn't good enough
and that's why you cheated on me.
Hell that was your own insecurities.

A shoulder to cry on is a dick to ride on, but not in my case.
When you found out about him you couldn't
Even stand the sight of my face.
Oh, I'm the bad guy now
Never even fucked that man, it's no way how.
But I'm foul for telling him about my dreams,
accepting complements and gifts huh?
Smiling and thangs

He made me feel wanted and beautiful again,
When my husband was paying me no attention,
Lost all interest in my ambitions,
even stop being my best friend.

When I'd be out to dinner with him
I'd be thinking about you.
When he tried to kiss me, I was scared as fuck
In self-defense to block his kiss I put both hands up.

See this is the difference between me and you.
I still long for your love and touch,
just any ol' penis will not do.
I want to make love to you, in my wildest dreams
I'm still fucking you.

You deflowered me and continued to water my petals.
I'm the lock to your key
and I really don't see no point of all the arguing.
But I can't Keep pretending that your indiscretions didn't hurt me.
I cannot forget
and forgiveness is nowhere in sight.
Two wrongs don't make it right,
Yet I wish you could feel an ounce of my pain.

Singing:
We don't have to live this way...
Baby, why don't you stay?

G

When I tell you I love you,
you know that I mean it,
He ain't a boxer
but I'm bobbing and weaving,
The main event,
we fucking all night to the morning surpassing the evening,
He going to lay that pipe like a plumber until I nut,
He nut we nut, we even.
I'm seeing the universe and his name ain't Steven.

I came in intending not to stay but,
he trapped me in his arms as we laid
He sleeping like a baby and I'm wide awake,
Being so close to his heart I can't really take it
I know what's at stake.
Had my heartbroken a time or two
the last thing I need is for you to rip it into two.

Your inconsistency scares me,
Not knowing where I stand from day to day
Week to week, month to month
oh shit we done hit well over a year
And the love I have for you is the type of love I fear.
That type of love that wonders where you are
And if 24 hours done passed
I want to pull up in my car
and check exactly where you are,

Who loving you and fucking you when I'm not around?
I'm from Spencer so you know how I get down....
This is what happens when you get my guard down
See when you were just someone to be seen,
Just another cat on my scene,
these type of things wouldn't even bother me...

3 a.m. I'm sneaking out
hair a mess but I got to bounce
Shoes near the door, jacket on the couch
Don't get up baby, I will let myself out.
One day he peeped the shit and said,
"Why you acting like this?
You get this good love then just dismiss
I thought we were better than this.

I'm no trick woman,
don't treat me like this
I've been hurt too
My heart been broken and walked on too,
I'm afraid are you?"

Hell yea I'm afraid,
maybe even more fearful than you.
Love has been a losing game for me,
I don't want to play it with.

"If I can hold on to you will you stay?"
I kissed him on his forehead then parted ways,
Made a long drive to my place
Looking back on that shit now
I realize what he meant that day.
He's sleeping like a baby, I'm wide awake
he trapped me in his arms as we laid.
As I adjusted my body I heard him say,
"If I can hold on to you, will you stay."

Wet Kanda Dream

He told me don't be afraid
as he swallowed the heart shaped herb.
He looked up at me purple veins seen.
His muscles were swelling amongst other things.
See I was merely an outsider looking for my roots.
Stumbled upon this magical place
Where I see all shades of my beautiful race.
He grabbed me by my hand and asked,
"How much do you love Wakanda!"

King I love Wakanda so much,
I dropped to my knees and begged him to stay.
He said, *"you are on your beautiful knees,
you don't have to do this please."*
But I'm merely an African American,
That's been feigning about some Wakandain dick.
I wasn't bold enough to tell him this.
I didn't even ask, I just pulled his robe up
Took his manhood into my mouth,
no hands while I gripped his butt.

He tried to send the Dora Milaje away
But Okoye said, *"no my King we must stay."*
He throw his head back
As I coated his manhood with my spit.
Hit the dick with two hands
what I call the slippery twist.
Judge me if you want,
but I'm an outsider that stayed,
Gave the best head of my life in Wakanda that day.
Wakanda forever!

Is It Me?

She was always the friend never getting any play.
If there were three of them and four of us,
She would always be ready to go
because she didn't get chose.
This is where her anger arose.
How come I'm never picked?
Seems like I'm labeled the ugly one in the clique.
Is it because of my body type?
Because I don't wear much make up?
Maybe it's my hair.
I don't get it, I'm just as educated,
dress just as well.
This shit been happening since we were kids.
We all were in the same circle
yet I felt like an invisible square.
Now we are adults and not much has changed.
Most of the squad married,
I can't even get a man to text back.
I'm wondering if it's me.
How can this be?
Y'all say I'm a catch
Why hasn't anyone caught me?
My friend you got to love yourself more.
It's you, it's definitely you.
A good man can smell the insecurities on you from a mile away.
Allow the inside beauty to make the outside too.

On The Set

I'm out here earning my stripes,
Day after day risking my life
but on the set my niggas love me.
I said fuck college because I got street knowledge,
The block is where I get my credits.
I'm out here pushing weight moving bricks like a construction worker,
Flex and I'll hurt yea,
On the set this shit in my blood
and moms know her baby a thug so I grind.
On the set I done had to plug a few niggas
I'm on some marksman shit with veteran trigger finger,
I'm cutting niggas down.
I'm untouchable,
my name in this streets strike fear oh you didn't hear,
On the set I'm splittin' wigs,
schooling these niggas like they my kids.
My bm's want me out the streets but they love the bank rolls more than me,
So we speak nothing but transactions when we meet,
I'm in the streets all day or up state,
But I'm steadily planting my seeds along the way,
On the set, who gone stop me, said who gone stop me?
On the set that's how I talked before they popped a G,
The homies found me
with my knowledge splattered all over the seats,
And guess what, them niggas left me,
I took my last breath alone, you feel me?
On the set I showed love every time I hit the street,
I caught bodies and charges for these niggas
Even allowed the weak to leach off me.
On the set who gonna take care of my moms?
On the set who going to be a father to my kids?
On the set who gonna help bury me?
Hell, I guess the SET ALREADY DID.

I'm in Need Of His Poetry

I'm in need of his poetry,
His words console me.
His play on words take a hold of me,
His metaphors never get old to me.
I'm in need of his poetry
It takes my stress away
and hugs my body tight,
Restores the smile to my face.
His stage presence brings peace.
When he spits something deep
the revolutionist awakens in me,
Ready to take on the world and anybody.

When he spits something romantic it sings to my heart,
From being to the end he has me in awe,
When he spits that erotic shit,
his words hit my woman hood
like a supersonic,
I'm dipping, mind flipping
imagining him putting the tip in....
ummm I'm in need of his poetry
it elevates and stimulates my mind.
I'm addicted
I'm in need of his poetry,
He's more than just talented,
He's gifted and not just anybody can spit what his spittin'
Rather it's to a beat or to pure silence
His words cut like swords
Every word will cut through your mind
He's a Poetic Black Samurai
I'm in need of his poetry,
I hope he's in need of mine.

Thief

You're a goddamn thief!
I was a fool for ever letting you in
You stole something more valuable than money
You are a deadly sin
See you stole my motherfucking time, that's a huge crime.
My intimacy and consistency is not to be toyed with,
You're supposed to be a man
but you still on that little boy shit
You robbed me of my focus
Damn I hope I didn't curve my soulmate,
While I'm playing this fairy tale fiction shit
Some damn hocus pocus...
Time is of the essences so how dare you waste mine?
Sending me false hope
playing with my emotions like I'm some joke,
When I move around you want to sulk
I get it, people play but watch who you playing with
My time is precious so watch how you taking it.
I don't want to hear that you're going to do better,
Hell, show me,
you've been wasting my time, shit now you owe me.
And since you can't give my precious ass time,
Do me this one solid favor,
stop ringing my damn line.

Tongue Tied

He said, *"wrap them legs around my head."*
My mother always taught me that, closed mouths don't get fed
Well hell, I hope momma taught you not to waste food,
because I'm about to give you more than a mouthful
Tonight I might break Steve Harvey's ninety day rule

Little did he know
The brother had me at hello
I was already undressing him with my eyes
and imagining him between my tights,
I used to have a height requirement
but this little ass giant, at heart, can jump the line
He can get on this ride any damn time.
He dipped his head, no mo' words were said,
Jesus must have been on the main line
'cause my soul left my body in no time

The way his tongue doing flips,
I'm gyrating and swaying my hips,
We both about to get a first class trip to ecstasy
Slaps sound like thunder clapping,
from all this ass he smacking
My my my whose son is this?
I'm about to write a letter to this man's parents
Hell, who shall I thank for this?
He already had my mind long before he had my body
He put some heavy shit on me mentally,
I couldn't tell anybody
Now he stroking it so deep
I want to keep my pace
but climax is written all over his face
This attraction started like a cat and mouse chase,
Now he is getting more than a taste.

Black Woman's Tool Belt

The word broken isn't reserved for black women only.
Anybody can be broken,
We forget that our man's hand also needs holding.
He is sick and tired of being sick and tired too.

Instead of saying "suck that shit up,"
How about saying, "I love you?"

What can I do to help you get over this hump?
A man is just a man when life lumps him up.
Ladies why do we not see broken,
in the eyes of our own?
When your king is down and out,
help return him to his throne.
Broken isn't just a word reserved for us.
Our men are suffering.

I be damn if we be the reason they suffer at home too.
Speak Life into him,
and watch our dreams come true.
A woman's love is the fuel that pushes our men through.
Help our kings see brighter days.
No down play on our sun rays.
Queen you are the LIGHT!
Forget the stereotypes lover we grinding.
Together forever the King and I.
I can see that you're broken and worth fixing,

So am I.

Universal Guardians

Dear Universe,
I won't let real love pass me by.
But could you protect my heart and time from that artificial love?
That love that is merely talk and no action.
That love that just never blossoms into something real.
That love that causes more frowns than smiles.
That love that isn't wrapped in love
and affection it's more like an infection.
Devouring time,
feasting on love that he never planned on giving back.
I'm strong enough to let my guard down.
But I'd hate to keep on being forced to put it right back up.
I won't let real love pass me by.
However,
I will allow that fake shit to run right past me.

Apart of your World

In order to be apart of your world I have to fit
If you say that I do, then you'll make room.
It's deeper than good morning texts and years' worth of sex.
All this time just keeps passing by and by
And your world still hasn't morphed with mine.
Tic tic tic boom
Can we address the elephant in the room or do we keep using an old broom to sweep it under the rug.
When kisses turn into peace signs,
Hugs turn into awkward space.
The smile you adored is no longer on my face.
When text messages stay on delivered
But Facebook posts are priority.
Guess I'm weird tho'
Just being a weirdo.
Wondering why the simple things are no longer the simplest thangs.
How much do we give?
'Cause now days,
Giving someone your best doesn't seem to be enough.
But when you turn your back on them here comes the fuss
What!
I'm not picking up your fucking crown,
Just for you to keep knocking mine off.
If we must go our separate ways, no love lost.

Inspirational Stroke

Fuck some inspiration into me
Put that dick in me
so deep that I can hardly speak,
and you just might be my motivation this week for dope poetry
He said I never heard your name in these streets
I'm mighty surprised by the way you speak
You look so innocent and sweet.

I am sweet,
sweet as the juices from a delicious peach.
Innocent, well I'm sure you're no full time angel either baby.
I bit my bottom lip,
as I slide my little brown soft hands into the front of his pants
And that dick was as hard as a rock,
Who needs the bed?

I want to see the shaking in his legs
While he tilts back his head,
'cause I have my mouth around his baby arm
Hell, I call it third leg.
His name isn't Kevin
but he opened my legs like gates,
Eating everything from the front to the back goodness sakes.
He comes up for air and he whispers in my ear
"This pussy the best thing I done had in my mouth all fucking day."

I licked his lips, he wasn't lying
I have to take back control of this situation
I climb on top I'm riding nonstop
He's begging me to stop
'cause he doesn't want to cum quick
but I'm enjoying this ride.
I don't want to hear that bullshit,
He grips my hips tighter,

he's lifting me higher.
I could go on and on how good this man boned.
Used to say he stays busy
but now he blowing up my phone
waiting on me to get home.

Damn guess that's the end of this poem.
Thanks Mr. Motivation
for being the inspiration for this poem.

Can't Get Right

You're absolutely beautiful, don't look away,
I seen the smile on your face and it's breathtaking.
Your entire being is amazing
and I'm just saying damn
How can this be that you are still on the market waiting patiently?
You're still full price no sale tag
and baby I'd spend my last.
Because this love will last longer than forever.
My soul shakes when you're near.
That love you got would make a thug shed the hardest tears.

Can I have you?
Don't look at me that way,
do you not hear the words flowing so effortlessly out my mouth?
Can I have you?
Not that half ass shit.
I want all of you.
Not that fifty percent, only infinity and beyond will do.

I'm going to whisper sweet everything in your ear.
Then yell it loud for all to hear.
Top shelf price with hypnotizing eyes
I cannot believe she didn't take you for keeps. Because literally you
wasn't shit with her because your soul was waiting on me.
Can't get right has now gotten it right.
I heard he never did that for she,
Well honey, she's not me
He didn't get right 'cause they wasn't right.
Not a bad thing at all
Because now you can fall head over hills for an unmarked lover.
That was sent to you from another.

Good Lotion

I caught him jacking off in the day time
He was all suppressed that I was home early embarrassed and shit,
I'm looking at the dick, dick looking at me,
I'm looking at the dick its well-endowed,
fully erect, not at all hard to see,
It started flopping and jumping, it's happy to see me,
I like dick tricks he got some skills,
I want to see how that day time dick feels.
My coochie throbbing I can damn near hear it through my jeans
He looked at me and said what you want to do,
Negro I'm already thinking about if I'm going to use one hand or two
Or no hands at all,
Instead just show you what this mouth do.
Spit, slur, grip, and spit
I'm going to town on that king dick,
I don't know what kind of lotion he was using
Thankfully it wasn't scented or thick
He already got the twitch as he grabs two hands full of my hair,
When I start to notice he got me really dripping, soak and wet down there
My focus is on this meat in my mouth
I'm done with fasting so y'all chill out,
removed my hands from his piece
So I can really get nasty,
His grip gets tighter, so does mine,
The pleasure might be his, it's also mine
He has no control
Like he is the submissive and I'm the Dominant,
Hell, he should call me master
Dick tasting a little salty so let me go faster
He busted that good nut
And I look at the night stand in disgust

"You used my good lotion!
Mayne WTF!"

Sunflower Amongst Roses

It's not easy being in love with you.
I feel like a flower that hasn't been watered enough,
The sunshine comes, I hardly ever get to bask in it.
Not sure if you even see me, like really see me
In a garden full of roses,
I'm just a sunflower trying to be marveled like a rose.

I don't have a place on the bush
I stand alone awaiting to be picked.
Time keeps passing yet
I still don't know what's in your head and heart.
Why are we still at start?
Ready player one? "Yes!"
Player two, player two, ready player two?
No not yet...still not yet.

I don't live in regret yet I feel like
My love you accepted
Now you reject it
And neglect
What happened to the
Our time is coming soon
I'm at peace when I'm with you
You say the same about me too

I don't get it
But I'm just a sunflower trying to be marveled like a rose
While others want to be Bonnie and Clyde
He and I are like Darius Lovehall and Nina Mosley,
Trying to figure this Love Jones out
Keeping our love and affection under wraps
Like people don't see the connection we got
But time is our enemy
When I want to just leave you be,

It's like damn he's a lover and friend to me
Both would end because
After all this time invested
Love has grown into something bigger
Than you and I
I guess you'll never be ready
Damn why aren't you ready?
Not sure if you even see me, like really see me
In a garden full of roses
I'm just a sunflower trying to be marveled like a rose.

A Queen Doesn't Have To Take

You're out here telling the world about him like he's yours
Just because you were giving up the pussy
Risking it all, doesn't mean a thing at all
You're old news I'm the new headlines
You thinking you're in competition with me,
Is the laugh of a lifetime

He must have that wood that will blow your mind
'cause you running around false advertising a relationship
like you done lost yo' whole mind
I don't like her, she took my man
I swear you hoes really just don't understand.
Queens aren't in the business of taking nobodies man,
We making men while you're forsaking and fornicating with them
You forgot the vows you've taken for another man
So help me try to understand

You're married, yet sleeping around
so why the fuck are you married now?
Riding every dick that's down
set that overly active pussy down
I can't be worried about the way you move,
But by all means honey, keep watching my moves.
See you probably caught him at a weak moment

I caught him at his best,
elevated on some God shit
I except nothing less,
my life requires peace not stress.
Now yo' lip poked out,
you mad and shit
I stole your man,
nah that's average chick shit
and the way you talking

I might not won't any parts of that sick,
He must have that pipe that will have your mind gone,
'cause he stay on yo' dome,
you blowing up that negro's phone.
Listen, Queens aren't in the business of taking men
We out here making men,
What part of this do you still not understand?

Painted Smiles

Oh she angry y'all,
just another angry black woman
Better yet an angry black bitch,
She has a huge chip on her shoulder
or one hell of an itch.
See Susan can be angry, Selena too,
God forbid that emotion comes from someone
who looks like me or you

How dare I be nothing but strong,
independent and cheerful?
The most unprotected person in this world,
And we are shown those words of Malcolm X
hold true every single day,
The world shits on me and I go get a degree,
Working a Corporate job
where the white man with little education
makes more than me

Because daddy owns the motherfucking company,
But I can't be angry
Won't fuck my way to the top
so I guess Brad stays on top,
My pay doesn't increase but it drops!
I'm walking and I'm attacked,
While my own men crowd and step back,
When we're on the front lines for you,
Thank you isn't needed, but way overdue,

I get it, I don't fit the description of the princess
who gets saved by the knight in shining armor.
Instead I'm taught to put on the oversized armor
and save myself and save you too
Because that what black women do.
Black girls are taught they don't need no man,

Everything they need they can get it on their own
protect your own solo throne,
Plus black men only want to fuck,
not cuff, so put yo' Vagina up.
But something in us are drawn to you,
When this bull shit holds true for a few,
We keep holding on to you,
But we're not allowed to be angry
when you leave us with your seeds
Turning us into what the world already foresees.

I can bare your children,
be your support system, and be your peace at night
But you'd be damn if you make me your wife,
I can't be angry so let me keep smiling,
I'm smiling,
still smiling hey do you see me smiling?

If I date outside my race I'm a bitter sale out,
If you date outside your race
you upgraded high fives and daps,
I'm a gold digger,
or she just a white washed bitch,
Slave mentality that's it....

I can't be angry so let me keep smiling,
I'm smiling still smiling, do you see me smiling?
I live for the day that the tide changes
and we don't have to be as strong,
We want love
and protection too as all other women do.
I have to be three times everything,
3x as smart,
3x times as pretty,
3x as charming
with not too much sass but still be friendly,
3x as strong because if he leaves
I have to keep carrying on

I have to be three times everything,

So why can't I be 3x as angry?
See Susan can be angry, Selena too
God forbid that emotion comes from me or you.
The world says fuck me

Apparently I'm supposed to smile and say thank you
Raped, discarded, damaged, and abused
I guess I'm supposed to smile
and say thanks for that shit too.
But let me keep smiling against all odds,
Like Black women are taught and forced to do.
Let me refresh my painted smile for you.

Make Up Sex

You talking all that
Blah blah blah
Like yo' meat game a sure thang
Hell, have yo' balls dropped?
Let me see how that thang hang
Do you got that pipe that can make a
Church girl sang
Do you play with the cat
'til it squirts on your shirt?

This a water fall
Not a sprinkler
Don't get yo' feelings hurt
You eat it right you might be a keeper
Don't shoot the messenger
I heard you fucked Tina
I give that win
She ain't got no kill
Are you ready for how great pussy feels?

She was running when you went deep in her
Well this a different type of ride
Hold on to both sides
I lift my own weight and grind
As I cream down yo' balls
I know you feel the juices flowing from these walls

Now don't pause
Don't freeze
In this moment you better please
Don't go buckling at the knees
Put your full lips on clitoris
My ovaries doing back flips like a gymnast

Your kids got to dripping down my tummy
Or be extra yummy
You can't cum up in this honey
But I'll bust on your tongue
I'm finished yea I'm d`wqone
I like all that blah blah blah
But this meow A1
Don't worry, that was just a test run

All poems and quotes by Sharita Renee

Sharita Renee

THE MIX
Evolution of the Pen & Pad

"You absolutely deserve the love you're trying to give to someone else.
Now keep that same energy when it comes to yourself.
Allow the beauty on the inside to be the best reflection of the outside.
I wonder whose loving you when you're forcing love on unworthy flesh.
You're the best part of most things, dope shit runs through your veins.
I just want you to get what you give.
So smile for me, please."

~Sharita Renee

"I'm cool with not having the stars, sun and moon.
I rather go to sleep and wake up each day knowing my heart is safe with you."

~Sharita Renee

*"It's the pride, the power,
the connection...
his entire being challenges me for
the better.
I vow to always be there to adjust
his crown when needed because
he dusted mine off and returned
it to my head before I had even
noticed it had fell.
Oh black king black king."*

~Sharita Renee

*"I see why she's idolized, the curve
between her thighs.
A real top shelf prize.
She is the light in the darkest of
places.
Yearning to be in close spaces with
her. She is woman, the giver of life.
All praises to the Most High."*

~Sharita Renee

*"She's going to get tired of meaningless text
and promises that are never met.
In tug of war who receives the most damage?
The one who keeps holding on and holding on.*

Telling their self just keep holding on, or the one that finally decides, I don't want to hurt anymore and let's go.

*See you're holding on only because I have yet to decide to let go.
You'd release the rope but you're too strong to go out like that.
Is that strength or weakness.
I'm just thinking..."*

~Sharita Renee

*"Don't plant insecurities
and doubts in people,
then wonder why it grows out of control; like wild weeds
in a beautiful garden."*

~Sharita Renee

*"He is broken,
so how many more wounds
and scars will you continue
to bare on your journey to
heal him and who will heal
you when the aftermath
leaves you broken too?"*

~Sharita Renee

*"We can't withstand the test
of time,
if we continue to test time.
People only do to us what we
allow.
So what happens when I put
my foot down?
Fearful of losing somebody,
who wouldn't shed a tear if
they lost you.
We are shedding,
out growing our old selves
and out growing what's not
meant to be."*

~ Sharita Renee

"Not all Kings and Queens were great beings,
yet they went down in history as great rulers nevertheless.

People don't always follow and praise you out of love.
Some do it out of fear, while others just follow because hell, everybody else is.
Ever wonder why we use the words king and queen so loosely."

~Sharita Renee

"Baby you don't have to make it so hard. In the process of protecting your heart you have to know in my hands it's safe keeps."

~Sharita Renee

"People be wanting friendship behavior
from people with associate mindsets."

~Sharita Renee

"Poetic, intelligent,
deliciously black...
who wouldn't fall head over heels
in love with that?
Mentally devouring my mind
with his thousand dollar words,
but you ask me why I can't let him
go...
The rhythm to my flow."

~Sharita Renee

My Mister

It's just uh another lonely night
Texted his phone "come hold me tight"
No reply 'cause he's always busy morning, noon and night
But that's alright
'Cause I told the universe
About him
She whispered in my ear "Love, don't doubt him."
I'm caught up in his whirl wind
My emotions doing backbends
Trying to be more than his homie, lover and friend
I was taught if you love it, lock it down
Don't leave no room for another to make her smile
With you I'm in the Nile
Floating in the river
Yo' touch makes me quiver
I will never be drained
I'm coming for the last name
If you don't wait too long
Might have babies and thangs
Body rocking to your beats, you stay bringing the heat
And I don't ask for much
So give me this one thing
Can I have all of you?
Not picture prefect but you're worth it
Your colors are true
So can I have you?

She Still Sleeps Alone

My body was in need of a healing.
I got a man, well kind of...
See he's only mine when it's convenient for him.
Love and affection seems to be to complex
And I'm too faithful so I go without sex.
Days and weeks, at times even a month plus once.
I deserve dick on demand,
Walks in the park holding hands.
I been a pro at keeping this secret.

I'm not into side dudes but in this case,
I should already have two.
One that lays pipe,
fucking and eating the pussy 'til he gets it right.
Side two is the date-night king and handyman.
Willing to play his position
'til a promotion becomes available,
Oh a huge plus if he is financially stable.
No worries he not pushing no other female's whip,
If you do give him some pussy just know he will be whipped.

See I kind of got a man,
So my fingers are strong
I know my body well so it doesn't take me long.
I want to run my fingers through locs, kiss bald heads,
Caress waves and the way these juices flow,
I can help that beard growth.]

Tonight somebody's son going to think I did time,
I'm just sex deprived.
I'm going to be wet at hello and climax by goodbye.
Boy I might have an orgasm
just from you touching my bare thigh.

Who Is Sharita Renee?

The Black Widow
I really don't need an intro
Pro black double stacked
Go ahead and google that
Poetically in love with words
In a three way with adjectives and verbs.
I give eargasms,
Make 'em cream before the scream...
Hey, cue the band the conductor
About to take the stand.
Black Prophet
You can knock it but
I guarantee you'll never stop it
P.H.D in flow
Master with the pen
Off the dome, should be a sin
Baby, I'm Swifter than the wind
it really don't matter the genre
I'm spitting in.
Black Hell cat I'm going in
Black soul
Dripped in gold
Made with the Black Gods mold
Blank Canvas my story has been written but never told
See my name in the poetic hall of fame
The black burning flame
Hallowed be thy name
SharitaRenee
Elevated the spoken word game
With her government name.

Misrepresenting

Bruh, she not looking for a dependent,
She looking for a spouse,
Stop acting like her son
and be the man of the house
Seeing is believing so stop running yo' mouth,
This lack of action going to have you out here ass out,
This isn't a refugee camp
Nor a homeless shelter.
You not in love my guy
you just a nigga seeking shelter,
And I can't help ya'

I'm not into all that extra,
I have kids,
gave birth twice and produced three
I don't remember you being none of the three
that came out of me,
Sorry I'm not raising you,

I can't baby you put up or shut up,
'cause I'm not phasing you,
Nor chasing you
I guess that's what them females of yo' past used to do.
Shit I pity the fool,
Because you won't pull the wool over my eyes
I see I caught you by surprise,

Maybe now you'll realize that talking like a boss
don't make you a boss
And I don't care how much your footwear cost,
You investing in your style
but don't have a home
or intellectual bone in your body

Yet running yelling you stunting on everybody,
nigga hardly
You still a boy misrepresenting a man,
You type of Negros I really can't stand.
Jumping from couch to couch
yet you the freshest dude out,
I can't figure you new Negros out,
All in the club buying bottles like you the plug,
asking every female for a hug.
I see you and I shoulder shrug,
I can't even hit you with a Church hug...
Bruh, she wasn't looking for a dependent,
she was looking for a spouse,
You're not her son
so get the fuck out of somebody else's mother's house.

Laugh Now Cry Later

You gave me something to believe in,
then slowly took it away
How can you be so calm
when lying in my face?
See you're the kind of man that's dangerous as fuck.
You seek good woman out,
Then fuck their lives up.

You appear to be prince charming
but you're really a Parasite.
Feasting off love
you have no intentions on giving back.
You're old enough to know better.
I thought your mother raised you right.
Thought grandma instilled greatness in you
Clearly something isn't right.

I fought for you, thought I seen a king.
My eye sight twenty twenty
So it's beyond me
Why you'd hurt me?
Maybe you're broken
Clearly damaged
Don't know loyalty

So being disloyal
is the only thing that rings your bells,
I want to yell go straight to hell!
Because I fell
Head over heels for you.
Your foul ass allowed me to.
Knowing I deserved better than you.
Blocked a real king's view.

You handled me all wrong.
I'm five miles to empty
My heart is running low
Instead of filling me up
You rather suck me dry
My cheeks are wet and you definitely know why.
Thank you
to this last man that made me cry.
You showed me way;
Being truly single
Is better than lying next to a lie.

Perfection Surrounded by Imperfection

In a world full of imperfection.
I allowed him to be perfection.
Because nobody's perfect but he makes me feel perfect,
don't have to tell him I'm worth it because he sees my worth.
I love him so much that it hurts.

Not that type of hurt that causes
Stress and pain.
Yet that type of hurt that makes you wonder,
What would happen if the unfortunate happened?
I want to grow old with him.
I have already made up my mind,
That in old age, if I have to wipe his ass
Then okay, fine.
Because he is mine.

We started this love race at a turtle's pace.
But with every day, every month
and every year that passes.
We get our footing right and speed up.
Not worrying about who passes us.
I just want to finish the race with you.

The trophy is effort,
The metal is the love.
But the Ultimate triumph is we made it together.
Against all odds and come whatever.

We built that strong friendship first.
The trust before the love.
Which fueled the process of falling in love
I just want to dance with him.
Make plans with him,
Build and expand with him.

In a world full of imperfection,
Together we are, our own perfection.

Christmas Gift

It was Christmas Eve,
Baby wanted to eat my Christmas treats.
I'm not going to lie,
His Eggnog is tasty and sweat.
I'm already thinking about hopping on his polar express.

I don't want a lot for Christmas.
He is a enough on any day
Just wait 'til these kids fall asleep.
Damn y'all go on to sleep,
So we can do the things that keep him
and me on the naughty list...
Year after year.

I'm going to deep throat his candy cane.
Suck his sugar plums because "tis the season
Hell ya'll know me,
I really don't need a reason.

I love on him all year long
and I know y'all say pussy isn't a gift,
but you've never had mine
and he fits me snug like Santa in his suite.
I spoil him with material thangs too.
This gift is to wet to wrap
He loves him some of my cookie,
but I'm nobody's snack.
A delicious holiday fest if we want to talk facts.

Sleigh bells ringing as love making turns into moans
and low muffled screams.
In the sheets I can be his ho ho ho ho.
Deep penetration,
Yet I still grab the small of his back.

Wishing he could go even deeper than that.

Having him begging me for more,
Kids done woke up knocking at the door.
"Momma is that Santa making all that noise!"
Why he in there with you.
"Santa play dead."
In my head I'm thinking,
if y'all mess up this nut
All that shit under the tree
I'm taking all that shit back.
I don't care if it's wrapped.

But instead I reply back,
Santa said go back to sleep.
He couldn't fit down the chimney.
So he came through my window.

Santa started to speak but I covered his mouth
And started gyrating my hips.
Will y'all go back to sleep,
Damn go back to sleep
Santa said don't peak at them toys and sorry for the noise.
Ain't no meat like the meat you have to sneak

Chessboard

You are so easy to love
Like a smooth melody your energy takes ahold of me
and I'm at peace
You are my personal stress relief
Outside forces have always been our issue
But the universe just won't allow anything
To keep us apart
You have been an Intricate
Part of this amazing puzzle
You just fit me
Body to body
our lips touch and stars align
Love like this is on the decline
Who loves you baby?
I do...
My life is amazing
and you add to my happiness.
Thank the most high you relieve my stress.
In the game of chess,
the Queen protects the King.
In life this is also a real thing.
I protect you by being your peace.
Before I ever gave you a piece
you had already became a part of me.
You are a part of my favorite love story.
Starring you and I

Orange Jumpsuit

People love to poke at a sleeping bear
Then wonder why they got mauled
I don't have words
All I got is hands
There is no wrath like the lords
Let God handle people
I'm sorry white Jesus
Must be on this mission
'cause he talking too damn long
Can we all just get along?
Fuck that
The same ones hollering love to jaw jack
My fuse done got short
I don't have the time or patience
For the back and fourth
Be the bigger person
Nah, I'm kind of short
Walking the Green mile
The hell I look like
John Coffey
I suggest you do your homework
and get up off me
My light switch on
And there ain't no off, B
Pray to the cross that you don't continue to cross me
No sleep for the wicked
Y'all never slumber
No naps
Coming back inconclusive like your last Pap
Don't make me snap
When I'm in my peace zone
Y'all can't leave me lone
Guess y'all trying to skip the line for that
Glory ride home

Shit Mixed Shit

You put me through some shit, and I mean that.
I know in life there's no take backs,
That's big facts 'cause you shitted on me.
Endured so much from the very beginning,
Losing far more than winning.
Yet I thought I seen a king, rubbed my eyes a few times
It was the craziest thang, still seen a king.
Now time done lapsed,
Lawd, dig me out of this huge hole I buried myself in.
You just had to fall in love.
Should have kept that shit to yourself.

My heart was bloody red now it's dark
and I won't be your friend.
Can't go back and I definitely won't play pretend,
A real friend would never hurt me the way you did.
Why the fuck did you even come for me?
Just to break my heart,
you probably knew you wasn't shit from the fucking start.
Yet, let years pass knowing you got me.
Fuck it my nigga 'cause now I'm snapping.
Master with the words,
Pretending you're a king, you do the shit so well
I didn't except a thing.
Gave me something I just can't give back,
it wasn't love tho',
So the pain will stick
Don't want to even cross your path.
I got to heal, it's my will.
Emotions make you cry sometimes, that shit is real.
Thanks to my poetry for allowing me to release.
Now that motherfucker is deceased to me
I wouldn't be me if I didn't leave you with one last thing
I wish you well, nah go to hell.

Go Fund Me

He called me out of breath
Said he was running from twelve
It's around twelve so,
I'm like what the hell?
It just never fails
Bruh I can't keep getting you out of jail
No I won't keep on posting bail

I can't keep being up at night
wondering if you are alright or worse
Have these cops killed you this time
I'm not ready to see your face on a T-shirt
Having females coming out the wood worth
Saying you was giving them that wood work.
See 'cause when you're gone,
That's when people want to ride your wave.
Put flowers on your grave.
But throw dirt on your name.
Don't be surprised how people change.

A hard head makes a soft ass.
Stop running these streets like you get a life time pass.
How much longer will this last?
Oh, until somebody cut you down.
So what's going on now?

Hello!
I said what's going today?
Because I don't have a place for you to lay.
Hello! Hello! Hello!
There was no reply.
A few hours later, knocks at my door.
When I see the red and blue lights,
I fell to the floor.

He called me out of breath.
I'm fusing not knowing that was his last breath.
Another go fund me page to be made

Woman to Female

"Hello, may I speak to Barbara?
Barbara, this is Shirley."
Pause!

See you won't get that type of woman to woman from me.
Shirley had to address Barbara
Then had to address her and Yolanda
And tell them both
You ain't woman enough to take my man

I'm really not sure why you'd put in the effort to come find me
I don't have the time to make fake social media pages,
and try to put pieces together about how you
and a man that clearly isn't yours is moving
Befriending me
Just because you see me getting embraced by a hug
By a man I'm guessing you love

I can't give you attention
Friend request deleted
because there is no competition
You running after him
and I can't I'm asthmatic
You blowing up the spot over him
and I call that ass backwards
You want to be Shirley that's fine
You can be Barbara too,
MVP of the sidelines
But I'm going to hit you with that Isha line
Because I'm not in the business of keeping a man
that don't want to be kept

Stop sliding in my DM dropping his name
You looking for some info

and ain't getting a damn thang
I'm the Queen
and you're the pawn in this here chest game
Shots fired and I'm aiming for yo' chest mayne
Straight to the heart.
Because now I know your weakness is this man
And that's what I will use to rip you apart.

Approaching me about him is some stooge shit.
I'm not curly, Larry or Mo hoe,
So get used to the way I flow.
Approaching me about any man is a no go
Be mad because I'm not biting your bait.
Asking about him, I and us
And you're willing to type
Message after message putting up this fuss
Only feelings getting hurt is yours

I'm laughing at your tactics,
As I listen to him snore.
On some woman to women shit.
You should never address another woman
Over a man that's supposed to be yours.
I don't never have to check you.
I run the shit to the one I'm lying next to.
You still waiting on my reply
Here it is

"Sis God bless you."

Woman to female that's how I address you

Mother May I

Before I came out my mother's womb,
I was already groomed to be a giver of life.
Three children but only gave birth twice.
The most high already knew I had it in me.
No there was no handbook,
it comes with the greatest joy but pain.
I'd put my life on the line for the unconditional love
and the wisdom I'd gain.

Every day I awaken
Teaching my children the skills they will need in this world.
Knowing one day I will be taken
but they will be prepared to make it without me.
My God I don't doubt thy.
Allow me to complete my mission,
Because ever since November 10, 2006,
I brought forth that beautiful being naturally
I felt like I could handle anything.
Oh you tested me Sep 2, 2011
I remember the doctor rubbing my forehead,
Telling me, *"You have done all you can do."*
We have to proceed with the C-section
It's a blessing, it's a blessing,

I had to keep telling myself woman it's still a blessing.
At twenty two weeks pregnant I had already risked it all,
To save their lives, highways and procedures.
It brought us to this point so let me dry my eyes.
Three months early please universe see us through.
Lawd if you allow my sons to make it,
I will never doubt you.
I evolved into a spiritual being during that journey.
The giver of life begging for my sons to have life.
A mother is more than a mother.

While bearing children we are so close to death,
While raising our babies we are willing
to battle the ripper in hand to hand combat.
We know these streets are unkind especially to our kind.

Mother may I,
be everything you birthed me to be...
As I break generational curses
and build a legacy that's worth it.
I have many titles
but being a mother is my most honorable position I possess.
It's exciting, adventurous and fun
but comes with great responsibility.

Mother may I,
Be as wise as the ancestors as I wear my crown proudly
Mother May I...
The universe whispered, *"Yes you may."*

Pedestal

Girl you put him on a pedestal
I hope he don't have you out here looking like a fool
You say it ain't the dick or what his mouth do
So what is it?

It's in his DNA
His genetic make up for goodness sake's
It's his array that got me wanting to stay
Hell it's the way he looks at me
When we are laying in the bed
and my legs are around him

The warmth of his body makes my heart beat steady
He confides in me about things that you wouldn't even believe
Things about his childhood that scared the shit out of me
I just want to be the reason he stops having nightmares
and starts having sweet dreams
I'm his good thing and he is mine

His mind is extraordinary
Ordinarily I'd be the teacher
but 60% of the time he schooling me
He is street smart, book smart
and everything in between

One day at the table he started to sing to me
Grabbed me by my hand
looked into my eyes
Girl I had to turn my head
My soul was screaming
Down South was creaming
My body was on fire
You know I have never been a lier

We didn't even get physical that night
He just snored in my ear and held me tight
So you right his meat game tight
His mouthpiece is top flight
But I'm in love with his mind
Captivated by his heart
Motivated by his being
Intrigued by his dreams
Yeah girl I put him on a pedestal
If he doesn't see the value in that,
then he is the damn fool.

No Wings: He begged me to let him fly

What do you do
when someone no longer wants to live?
The pain is too much,
I don't want to be here,
and you don't know how I feel,
Until you have lost a sibling or a parent,
you sympathize with me, I don't want to hear it.

I want to fly,
I need to meet my loved one beyond the sky.
You don't get it,
they say joy cometh in the morning
But mornings have come
and gone and where is my joy.

I want to fly,
let my feet no longer be on the ground
but scrapping the sky.
I don't want to live, I want to die
I'm tired of you asking me why,
I can't cope, I have no hope, and all I do is cry
I try to shake these thoughts but they catch me,

Why did God have to take the best thing in my life?
I wasn't ready for that phone call that night,
I didn't even get to say goodbye,
I want to fly because I don't sleep at night,
But I'm looking forward to my dreams that never come
Because that's the only time he talks to me,
You say I'm grieving and things will get better,
hell it's almost a year...
A year full of tears,

Why won't you let me fly?
It's not getting any better
You keep saying look to the hills for my help
But I'm in the dark
and nobody's here to light my way...

I want to fly,
he wants to, but I won't allow him to
and y'all know why....

Family in the Sky

You left and we stayed
Family gatherings and BBQ's will never be the same,
Who will bring the lemonade?
Who will get drunk as a skunk
and start to sang *Summer Rain?*
Things are forced to change

The leaves of our family tree are steady falling
Family in the sky I'm calling on you
Reflecting on the things we used to do
Remember when great grandma used to play the blues,
and tell grown folks gossip
We called that news

Uncles and aunties loud talking while playing bones,
A fight broke out but nobody's going home
The good old days when y'all dwelling was here
And death wasn't something we feared
Who will dance all night
under the stars like papa used to do?
We'd party all night to the song,
Blue Suede Shoes
What I wouldn't give for one more kick back night?

My family in the sky would get the first invites.

Three Way

She said she wants to be the sheets in this three-way meet,
Baby said it was a fish fry so he'll bring the meat.
As legs spread I don't know what's ahead
Thoughts running wild tongue in the butt I won't decline,
Cum dripping down my spine,
It's a pussy platter, so wear a bib it might splatter.
My Sheba stay wet, I never doubt her.

I hope she ain't a screamer because baby lays pipe deep.
He darts that tongue in and out,
have you doing that church goers shout.
We don't invite many into our bedroom boom
because our fucking can become addictive.
It will have you doomed.
You're heart and pussy will fall victim too soon.

So disclosure because we won't be to blame
Hopefully swallowing kids is your thang.
Weekend get-a-way's every blue moon,
we might hit you up,
If we don't then we don't, so don't put up a fuss.
It's a freak thang, and sometimes we let it out.
This is our little secret shhh don't blab it out.

Are you cool with the rules?
This is what our three ways are about.
I'm a pillow princess, so yo' pussy I won't eat.
But I promise if you eat mine y'all crave it in your sleep.
Climb in these sheets and begin the feast.

Fatal

The fatal attraction
The dramatic distraction
Didn't bear any consequences to their infractions
But the one that chilled did
The same one that played her position
Never letting anyone know her mission
How your face in this kitten,
I don't have to mention
I'm tatted up
but have no intentions on adding your name on my canvas
Without a husband title?
Hell stop the madness
She must be insane
I won't pop up to blow the spot up
That ignorant shit ain't love
Emotional roller coasters but you don't know Love
Lying then lying then lying, doesn't equal honesty bruh
Honestly, honesty can get you far
There are many ready to play a part
Don't let that feeling shit have you feeling shit that ain't real
You got some good dick but let's be real
Only weak minded chicks fall in love with just dick
That's pure clown shit

Hell on Earth

How long will you allow it?
How many nights will you cry?
When will a push turn into a punch?
Foundation and cover up
won't cover the mental damage
that next choke could be your last

You're talking out your ass
not wanting to put the laws on his ass
You reach out to family
We ain't having none of that
So when we show up don't tell us no now, bag back
Saying The Lord will handle him

Ummm, I don't have that time
so my hands will do just fine
I can't stand a nigga that will knuckle up on a woman
But won't dare step to another man
I see the bitch in you nigga
And bitches I can't stand
You ain't no damn man

Other women justifying your behavior too
Just because they share the same bloodline as you
Maybe somebody's son will beat they ass too
You can pray all day for someone to change
Some people are filled with this evil rage
I can't waste my prayers on a man like this

How long will you allow all this?
When slaps become closed fist?
Or when the next victims are your kids?

Wake up sis!

Yelling, wake up!
She will never get up again
now my mind is all messed up
We allowed this monster to walk amongst us

All That Talking

If you're nasty just show me,
Don't brag on your dick
talking all that shit,
When we're alone you're folding
Sis he asking for the pussy and shit,
So I play it off like,
nah move back up little homie,
stranger danger in this bitch
We done already established that it's yours,
If you have a key
then why you knocking on the door.
Play fighting and shit
that dick as hard as arithmetic,
But you not doing shit

Hold me down,
demand me to set on my hands
While my pussy meets your tongue and they slow dance.
Don't ask me what you can and can't do,
I will let you know if you're doing too much baby
Knowing me shit, you ain't doing enough

My back is arched
and that's your cue
to slide that dick in this pussy
Don't forget to put your thumb to work to
You asking what you can do,
that's a turn off for me
I'm not obeying too many sex boundaries

If I want the dick guess what?
I'm taking that shit
This isn't rape it's mine
I got my name on that shit.

So when I pull your pants down
and I'm giving that neck,
Its sloppy don't try to stop me,
I'm sucking the dick
not neglecting the balls,
Your legs are shaking please don't fall,
Something like the coach and I got you by the balls
So be prepared when I get up to beat down these walls
I'm not asking you to allow me to throw it back,
If I have to tell you one mo' time to smack that ass
you not getting a call back.
You don't need permission,
might have to fuck me into submission.
It's yours right, so fuck me like theirs no competition,
and when you bust that nut oh no sir we ain't finished.
Gone rest your eyes, then get back in this.
You just started now, finish!
You were doing all that talking.

Return My Heart

I made the decision today that I want my heart back.
Leave it at the door broken and wounded.
I will take on the task or repairing it myself, again.
Exit left please.
You are a pro at being ghost.
When I need you the most, you're never there.
Your bailout game is on the highest level.
My heart can't take any more pain,
So it's pedal to the metal.
You want love that you are too damn selfish to give back.
You want loyalty that you don't possess.
Do you realize that I damn near lost me behind you?
Pushing dreams to the side that's artistry suicide.
So damn it, leave my heart.
I said leave my heart.
Don't you dare take it with you, y'all have to part
I rather bleed out on the MIC.
Allow the claps, snaps and screams to heal me.
My own words to stitch me up.

Somebody Else's King

He called me this morning out the blue
Said he could feel my pain in his sleep
I'm not sure how to respond because
This man isn't mine
Yet he is always on time

A shoulder to cry on
Yet never a dick to ride on
I could never risk our friendship like that
Please, I'm no home wrecker
And that's true facts
He has always nurtured my BLACK

Stays having my back
He is beautiful black
He restored the image
I have about black kings
Sometimes I catch myself looking at his ring
Smiling because I know he treats his wife like a Queen

In return
I pray she's giving him everything deserving of the world
But would give it right back
He pulled me up by my boot straps
Told me the game
Displayed what a black man should be
Damn he elevated the game

He is the prototype
As I type I want to cheer for him
As corny as it sounds
Every word he says is so profound

He could feel my pain

Even when I didn't want him to
The King has told me so many times
To leave dude

I tell him he just doesn't understand
Although he is also a man
He replied but not every man
Is ready to take the grand stand

Why give him a throne that's too large for his ass?
Why build him a home
then give his weak ass a hall pass
I'm not trying to bash
But you shouldn't have to ask
Somebody to make time
That takes time

I felt your pain in my sleep
Sis did you feel mine

Let's Grow Old Together

Since we can't live in the moment
let's create more moments,
Moments that will last us a lifetime
And hold us over
until we are in each other's presence again.
I need that overflow of love.

See if old age takes anything from me
I hope to God it's not my memory
I have too many Precious memories of you and me.
Way too many but I don't want to forget any.

You have a hold on me
and I want you to grown old with me.
I have already decided that I'm here to take care of you.
When you're sick I want to give you a healing
I don't care about all that jazz you spillin'.

Rocking outside on the porch
watching our grand babies run around
They don't realize just how long GG and papa been down...

Bloody Words

Phone calls in the night
My gut feeling tells me something definitely isn't right
The first thing that comes to mind
is I hope it isn't my brother
Then I look at the time
it reads 4:49am

I grabbed my phone to say hello
All I hear is screams, then a light beams,
I peep through my thick blinds
Who the hell could be coming by at this time?
The screams from the phone became distant,
Then the call was dropped or just ended.
Hard knocks at the door,

I grab the nearest garments and threw them on,
As I approach the door
still holding on to my phone...
Two women were there,
I can't make out their faces,
They both have dazed looks on their faces...
"Ms. Sorry to wake you but do you know this man?"
She shows me a photo on the phone in her hand

Yes I do but we haven't spoken in months,
When he calls I never pick up.
We had a huge fall out,
Right now it escapes me what about,
I was dealing with him, what's up?

Well that's our brother and our best friend,
Do you think you can let us in?

Come on in.

That's when the air became thin
Why are they here?
What is this all about?
That's when one sister pulls a bloody note out
to be continued...

Day Dreaming

He said I can see his dick print from space.
Told him my sight ain't what it used to be.
He said what about your taste?
Fuck that half of chub,
Allow me to make space.
So you can bust on my face
And have room for that ten inches to lay.
It's a fucking race.
Keep up your fucking pace.
Eat it from the back
And I might cream on your tongue.
Tsunami on your face.
Devour me like a country boy
And I just might run.
Hope your dick game is just as fun as that tongue.
I can pick that dick out of a line up.
Said he a freak so go ahead and toot that ass up.
Slid me to the edge of the bed.
Choke me with one hand,
While you beat it up.
We collapsed in a pool of mixed nuts.
Started with a dick print,
Ended with a nut.

Carnivorous

She's only happy when she's laying under a man
Any man will do
Sis not complete without the meat
It's an addiction and she weak

I'm giving y'all a sneak peek,
this has nothing to do with being a freak.
I have known her longer than most.
Yet I only remember two or three relationships she was in.
Like on some,
This baby, oh this my man.

Sixty plus body count,
I hope she cuts that shit out.
Once she started forgetting negros names
but could recall how many times he came.
Revolving door,
bathroom floors a self-proclaimed modern day whore.

Ain't no peace like his piece.
No thrill like the feel of that pleasure and pain.
Love has always been a failed mission.
She said she doesn't feel,
I can body and bounce, no feelings, not an ounce.

Hey, that's what they do to us.
I don't have time to fuss, cuss or care enough.
Give me my fix, my dealer is that dick.
I don't want to be fixed.

Earthly Father

My father taught me that,
We make time for who and what we want to make time for,
So if he can't make time for you
then baby girl he isn't the man for you...

A successful man is a busy man
A successful man in his right mind,
Will make that time to also nurture his relationship with you.

My pops be on some of that real shit

*"See baby girl, I treat you like God's gift
because you are God's gift to me,
I can't have God's gift in the hands of just any old body,
That's satisfied with putting his hands on every damn body
He has to be equipped mentally and spiritually,
You can walk around like a king
But if you're still doing peasant things
then your title don't mean a thing.
You're not just looking for a ring,
You're looking for that cloud nine feeling that true love brings,
His last name won't mean a thing if his love isn't everlasting,
I say this with passion.
I know it's hard for you,
'cause you grew up beautiful country and kind of green,
You see beauty in people that most have never seen.
Men have hurt you and this hurts me
because my little princess is a black Queen.*

*You're a butterfly,
don't allow anyone to clip your wings,
If you keep doing what you're doing,
You will have you something better than a king.
You are God's gift to me, so I treat you like God's gift...*

Only another God can treat you better than this.

You can feel it in his kiss,
Remember your earthly father taught you this."

Good Enough

Good enough to nut up in.
But not worthy enough to put a ring on.
Amazing enough to string along.
But not dynamic enough to give a title to.
You don't love me, you're addicted to what I do.
You're in love with the juice
An addict for the grip
Mesmerized by the hips.

See that's why I made you wait so long
because I wanted the love for me.
Remember that jazz about you wasn't in it for some ass.
You wanted a love that would last
But right when you got it,
Look at yo' ass.
I'm about to spazz.
I need to detox from yo' black ass
And no, you're not getting a pass

Because I had been healed.
Was finally ready to get back in the dating pool and swim.
But before I could even get my feet wet you came along.
Made it easy to like you
but you didn't come on too strong.
Time doubled up on us.
What I have for you is love
And what you have for me is lust.
This shit got me wanting to fucking cuss
I should have known,
got me questioning was I good enough.

I wish she had a dick

She asked to take my pain away
As her soft hand creased my face
This goddess said
You don't need no man
Plus no man can do what I can
I use my tongue for pleasure not for lies
This guy crazy for taking you on a foul ride
I can heal you better than he can
Make your body scream louder than he can
Making you smile all over is my plan

She was 5'9
Beautiful dark brown skin
Hazel eyes you could swim in
A heart big enough for you to live in
She had been asking me to switch sides for years
Had even been the one wiping my tears

I put it to her sweet
Yo' pussy my dear
I'm not about to eat
I love dick
My diet all beef
Fish might be healthy
but it's not on my plate

Before I could say anything else
she put her hand between my thighs
Whispered don't worry I'm skilled
I deep sea dive
I need to taste your juices
and show you how this mouth to south do
Not here for anything other than to please you
She went

Down
Down
Down
Flipping and dipping that tongue
Head game so fire
Didn't know if I should shed a tear
Thank Jesus
Or run

Inside my head I envisioned
She was just a beautiful man
And had myself some fun
Threw my head back as she bath my cat
My hands full of her hair
I hope she didn't think I was a snack
If she had a dick I'd throw it back
I can feel it all in my back

She sloppy with her tongue
I can feel juices flowing down my crack
Like we left water running
Legs shaking
ASS clapping
I busts on her pearly whites
It was only right

See came up looked at me
I'm looking at she
As she wipes her chin and licks the cream
She continues to look at me
And says so you know what these means?
I bite my lip
I reply not a damn thing
Unless we adding a dick to this thing

F**k Your Brother

See you playing a lot of games
That's cute,
oh that's sweet
But you'll be calling me sis the next time we meet
See I'm not one to play games
Be low or sneak
but you got me kind of twisted my G
See when I play the game I play for keeps
All that little shit you doing seem hell of weak
So peep,
I'm going to do some shit that's going to shake your soul
Bitch, hunt you 'til your old
I forewarned you baby this shit done got old
Im'a fuck your brother,
But I'm going to take my time
See I'm with the shit
So I'm going to get into his mind
Don't worry you'll be calling me big sis in no time
Remember you love my honesty,
so the pleasure is all mine

Fucking or What?

I aim to please
So all this talking need to decease
So my witness can increase
You can use your tongue to lick the wetness dripping from me
He want to chill, I want to fuck,
He want to talk I want to nut!

Please baby please,
Shut the fuck up
He like it slow
I want a combination of that slow motion and fast
I like to be in front of the mirror
While he smacking my ass
While giving my cat a tongue bath

Oh no zadaddy
Keep the lights on
I want to see that strong,
Long dick going in and out,
Let me enjoy the ride while I'm bouncing on your lap
and your begging for a quick nap.

I aim to please
Don't worry about me baby
I have strong knees
This opportunity I must cease
Don't cum off just the head
It's not intended to put you to bed.
I'm still in my prime so legs can fully spread.

I aim to please
I know you don't have a round two in you
Looking at his ass sleep smh
Like what I'm going to do with you?

Head game kind of cocky
Hope he has a towel on the night
Cause it's going to get pretty damn sloppy
He going to have to wipe his ass
two hands or none
I do this for my pleasure too that's what makes it fun.

By five am that dick will magically,
like clockwork get hard
I will slide my fingers down south
to give myself a jump start.
I aim to please
So pleasing you is pleasing me
You might be still kind of sleep
'No Cardi B' I'm going to get that D

Said that's what he loves about me
I aim to please, no need to doubt me.
He digs my mind and my poetry
He's in my thoughts during *Dope Poetry*.
Pussy wetter than the ocean he exploring me,
he's parting cheeks and spitting in between,
that's deep sea driving like a G
if you know what I mean

I aim to please
I'm sucking his dick not neglecting the balls,
Spit and my juices coating his dick
I lick it off like applesauce...
She aims to please
I am she
So bust those sweet dick juices
all over my pearly whites,
Exfoliating my skin this is a win win
I aim to please

I'm Gone

She's not here to be your step stool
Lapdog might be an understatement
She is the Queen and not the servant
Don't get it mistaken

It's her dynasty to be your partner in crime
Yet you can't keep wasting her damn time
It's no feeling like feeling free
No cage bird
but lock me down

Straighten my crown don't knock it down
Be the reason I smile and not frown
Cause I'm telling you right damn now
When I'm gone I'm gone

Not easily broken
but hard as hell to leave alone

I'm gone!
Dynasty just called and I answered the phone
I'm gone!

Something About His Eyes

I found peace in his eyes
Long before he ever got between these thighs
Our wild love ride had no GPS
Tho' it brought some stress

I took it as the test,
That I've been trying so damn hard to pass
He sings my hearts love song
Can we make it last?
Just let love win

Can't bare to lose my lover and friend
We won't go back
Nah can't go back
I'm going to demand my heart back
Just stating facts

It's not on you baby it's in you
Trying hard not to end me and you
So help me
Don't change for me change for you

I can imagine life without you
and I don't like that shit one bit
The boyish stuff you do, you need to quit
Yea I talk big shit

But having to walk away from you
will be the hardest thing I've had to do
I was made for you
Act accordingly so we can live our forever

According to God's will
Man you make me feel like

Late nights and early mornings
Making love on balconies

While I'm begging baby deeper please
My dope and stress relief
It's you and me
Me and you
Don't let naysayers prevent greatness boo

Meat Delivery

She mad because she don't got consistent dick
And when he do drop that dick off
he nuts hell of quick
This ain't that petty pussy
This top of the line!
My pussy got a nickname
He call it big fine

Life is too short for wack sex and bad ass convo
I want to fuck you in the parking lot
Drop the mic let's go!
She has morals
but her pussy wants to be a hoe
Ride down on him
and if he good he get that steady flow
If the head and dick trash man excuse me,
I got to go
I think they confused
on how a relationship suppose go

Dick on demand,
shouldn't have to command
My sex drive in over drive
you clearly don't understand
I swear everybody in the world fucking but me
at least that's what me and my fingers think
I tried to louts myself on that fake meat
damn near broke my feet!
That's a two person job I fucking think!

All the remotes missing batteries
Too proud to beg but I like to be on my knees
Mouth open waiting for the cream
Don't talk about it be about it

Fucking me into submission, doubt it
But I'm up for the challenge.

You know what? Forget it
Where his sister at?
I haven't worked myself up to eat the cat yet
Can I just be a pillow princess?

Point me in the direction of something soft on the eyes
She can be about 5'5
That will scissor me 'til I almost cry
she needs to like big butts
Black beauties with tasty ass nut

I promise I will work up the confidence
to eat the pussy up
Cross My figures behind my back
I kid I kid
She just mad because
She doesn't get consistent dick.
That's it

The Great

He is one of the strongest men I know
Always a king at work
You can tell the greatness in all of his work
Putting family and friends before himself
He barely has time to focus on self

I admire him
He is one of the *GREATS*
Complemented by the sweetest taste
In his arms is my safe place

In my heart there's a special pure place just for him
He touched my very soul
Yea, we have been through a lot
But we push through
The Most High made me for you

We are a part of this unique design
And ever since you put your hand in mine
I knew I wanted to spend time
I'm talking about a few forever's

Wishing my firsts could of been with you
But my lasts will have to do
I will wipe your tears
Help you face your fears

Root you on from the stands
I'm his number one fan
Yelling is there a heart in the house tonight?
Well baby I have already stood up

I vow to be your backbone when you don't feel as strong
To be the sweetest lyrics over your prefect beat

I can't promise we won't go through somethings
But I can give you my word,
If we allow love to win we will make it

Our love they can't take it
That's my shawty
Amongst so many other things
I hope he knows he means the world to me

About the Author

Who is Sharita Wilson, AKA "Sharita Renee?"

Public speaker, poet, author, passionate about black youth and empowering people from all walks of life, ethnicities, and ages. She has been a featured poet at many events in Oklahoma City, such as *Poetry and Chill OKC, Dope Poetry Night, Souled Out Sundays,* and the *Poetic City Slam,* just to name a few. She has also spread her influence beyond the borders of Oklahoma, performing at events like "*Hotter Than July*" (Tulsa,Ok.) *"Blacknificent"* (TX) , and "For the Love of Poetry (TX.)

Although she loves poetry she is also set on improving mental health literacy, not only in her community but nationwide. Volunteer work is apart of her growing platform. She is always looking forward to working with non-profit organizations.

Sharita Renee believes that charity has no off season. She holds the position of Mental Health Specialist at one of the leading healthcare facilities in the Metro, and is also furthering her education at Oklahoma State University. The captivating works of her poetry have graced stages and radio; now she is on her journey as an author. From poetry, short stories, novels, to children books, Sharita Renee is ready to publish something amazing for all the readers of the world.

Copyright © 2019 Sharita Wilson.

All rights reserved. No part of this publication may be reproduced, distributed, or transmitted in any form or by any means, including photocopying, recording, or other electronic or mechanical methods, without the prior written permission of the publisher, except in the case of brief quotations embodied in critical reviews and certain other non-commercial uses permitted by copyright law.
For permission requests,
email BenniePublications@gmail.com
or contact Sharita Wilson.

ISBN: 978-0-578-47770-1
Library of Congress Control Number: 2019908347

Any references to historical events, real people, or real places are used fictitiously. Names, characters, and places are products of the author's imagination.

Front cover image by *Designs by Demarco.*
Interior photos by *Marius Lee Photograpghy.*

Printed in the United States of America.

First printing edition July 2019.
Bennie Publications LLC.
Benniepublications@gmail.com

Facebook

Poetic Greatness By Sharita Renee

Poetic City

Instagram

Sharita_Renee

&

Poetic City

Youtube

Poetic City

Acknowledgments

First I must give honor and praise to *The Most High*.
I'm here to do your will, by your grace I'm still here.

Who would I be without my loves
Kyla, Donatella and Cerventes?
I hope you guys are proud of mom. I love you beyond words.
For understanding that poetry is my passion and job.

Special thanks to my parents,
Marcus and *Thomasena Dumas*.
My siblings *Tanisha Wilson, Marcus Dumas*;
My best friend/sister *Monick Braggs* for your endless support.

To my friend *Shayla,* for pushing me to finish by any means.

Marius Lee and *Cordney McClain (Mac Woods)*
you both spoke words into me that manifested into power,
appreciative for your wisdom and friendship.

Dope Poetry family, *Poetic City* tribe
and others that have allowed me to grace the stage and level up;
I'm grateful and humble.

Tavie the Poet,
for the opportunity, you sparked something within me.
Blessings to you.

Bennie Publications,
this book wouldn't have had the same effect without the passion
Joelisha Goggins brings, Salute Queen.

Last but never least, to the king that seen the evolution of my pen
and pad when I was still wearing blinders, thank you my love.

Thank You!

www.ingramcontent.com/pod-product-compliance
Lightning Source LLC
Chambersburg PA
CBHW042308150426
43198CB00001B/6